12 RULES FOR STUDYING

A MUST-READ FOR EVERY STUDENT

RENELO PEQUE

BALBOA.PRESS
A DIVISION OF HAY HOUSE

Balboa Press books may be ordered through booksellers or by contacting:

Balboa Press
A Division of Hay House
1663 Liberty Drive
Bloomington, IN 47403
www.balboapress.com.au
AU TFN: 1 800 844 925 (Toll Free inside Australia)
AU Local: 0283 107 086 (+61 2 8310 7086 from outside Australia)

Because of the dynamic nature of the Internet, any web addresses or links contained in this book may have changed since publication and may no longer be valid. The views expressed in this work are solely those of the author and do not necessarily reflect the views of the publisher, and the publisher hereby disclaims any responsibility for them.

The author of this book does not dispense medical advice or prescribe the use of any technique as a form of treatment for physical, emotional, or medical problems without the advice of a physician, either directly or indirectly. The intent of the author is only to offer information of a general nature to help you in your quest for emotional and spiritual well-being. In the event you use any of the information in this book for yourself, which is your constitutional right, the author and the publisher assume no responsibility for your actions.

Any people depicted in stock imagery provided by Getty Images are models, and such images are being used for illustrative purposes only. Certain stock imagery © Getty Images.

Print information available on the last page.

ISBN: 978-1-5043-2450-2 (sc)
ISBN: 978-1-5043-2451-9 (e)

Balboa Press rev. date: 02/02/2021

This book is dedicated to my Creator

THANK YOU

To all my family and friends

The good friends I met at Aarhus University in Denmark

The University of Melbourne (where I did accountancy
bridging courses and Information Systems)

Deakin University (where I completed Bachelor of Laws)

Aarhus University (where I completed Climate Law)

College of Law (where I completed Practical Legal Training)

The University of Notre Dame (where I
commenced Master of Laws)

CPA Australia

RENELO PEQUE
Certified Practising Accountant
Admitted to the Supreme Court of Victoria as an Australian lawyer, 2020

12 RULES FOR STUDYING

Please read this before everything else

This introduction gives you a context of why and how these 12 rules for studying were developed. Once you understand the rationale, you can modify some of the 12 rules in this book to suit your circumstances. If I were to list in detail all the techniques and strategies I used and learned from other people, there would be around 50. However, no one wants to read 50 techniques or rules. I certainly don't want to write 50 rules for studying, so I came up with a solution. I went through the techniques and strategies and distilled them into their essential purposes. I used those purposes to identify the principles behind them. Once I understood the principles, it was a lot easier to write the rest of the book because I knew what the techniques are aiming for. Once I managed to narrow down the list to 12 rules, I thought that's a lot easier to digest than going through 50 items on a list. You want study techniques that you can easily understand and implement straight away. The principles eventually became the three categories of the 12 rules. The categories are preparation rules, effective strategies and memory enhancers. As there are four rules under each category, it was more manageable for me to focus on one category first before moving on to the next one. As a reader, you may also want to focus on any one category at a time. For example, you can jump straight to the second category because it relates to actual study techniques rather than going through the preparation rules which are more about your physical and mental conditioning. It's up to you.

The implementation of the rules may be different based on your environment and area of study, but the underlying principles are the same.

I decided to take up law after a number of years of full-time employment while also running my own business on the side. I was always busy. I still am. During the course of my employment and business engagements, I became interested in many of the legal aspects of my work. I would often look up meanings of legal terms and analyse them. I read about taxation, contracts, corporations and employment law. As I got more exposure to legal matters, my curiosity of the law grew. When I did my accounting degree, business law was one of my favourite subjects. I even got 100% in one of the examinations. At the back of my mind, I knew that eventually, I was going to pursue a career in law.

Aside from full-time employment, I pursued other things like learning musical instruments, writing books and eCommerce.

Instruments. I learned to play the guitar in high school with my friends. It was the first musical instrument that I liked to play. I still play it. I tried playing the piano for a couple of weeks but I didn't particularly like it, so I stopped. I also learned drumming which came natural to me even during primary school. I would tap my desk to song beats. People would call it pen tapping or desk drumming. One summer, I decided to join a youth camp. A band played on the first day. The next day, I woke up and headed straight to the stage where the musical instruments were. My friend, whom I met at the camp the day before, picked up the guitar and I picked the drumsticks. We jammed. It was the first time I played the actual drum kit. My new friend asked me how long I've been playing drums. That's when I realised that I was good at it, so I pursued drumming. Years later, I became a drummer of a local band in Melbourne. We went to different schools and churches to perform. I also became a drummer of a Christian Church in Melbourne. After playing drums for a number of years, I decided that I was going to learn a new instrument. I thought about the saxophone and Kenny G, so I watched a lot of videos of great saxophone players. I was inspired. I started learning on my own through YouTube until I accidentally met a saxophone teacher. I thought this must be destiny because I was just starting to learn how to play the saxophone and this guy showed up. I was called to be a saxophone player! I said it too soon because after a few weeks he stopped coming without notice. That first weekend that he didn't turn up, I thought something important probably came up. He never showed up again the following week and the week after that. I decided to continue learning on my own. However, I had to stop when I started law school.

Books. Yes, I wrote two books before this one, one related to accounting (boring and uninteresting to most people) and another about weird things people do on the train (definitely not boring). I went from being serious to being comical. Some people said that I was ruining my reputation as a professional person because all of a sudden, I was writing a book about weird things people do on the train. They said that my actions and projects needed to be consistent with my profession to build my reputation in the industry; and that the comical book might convey a wrong message to clients and prospective clients. In the end, the book was published. My professional life wasn't affected.

eCommerce. I started a mystery gift website where you buy a present for yourself or someone and you don't know what it is. We chose the gift for you based on the recipient characteristics that you provide such as gender, age and interests. That business failed. I also started an apparel business, mainly T-shirt. It also failed. Later on, I started another T-shirt business with a new logo. It also failed. Eventually, I decided to focus on my accounting business.

When I went for a holiday in the Philippines, my auntie, who is a lawyer, encouraged me to take up law. She shared her experiences, the ups and downs, the joy and the pain of being a lawyer. I thought a lot about all the things she said. When I got back to Australia, I started inquiring about getting into law school. I found a good university offering an off-campus option. I applied. I waited. I got accepted. I didn't have to quit my job.

The classes were due to start in about four months. I had to put some of my projects on hold such as learning the saxophone and eCommerce.

Fast forward to 2019, I completed my Bachelor of Laws in November after four years of juggling studies and full-time work. I still managed to have a social life during this time and stayed in touch with family and friends. I also managed to get into an exchange program with Aarhus University in Denmark and travelled to 13 cities in Europe. I learned a lot about those cities, their people and culture. I also made new friends. Even with all the travelling and my activities, I still managed to have four 'Distinction' subjects. If it weren't for the tools and techniques that I have developed over the years, this would not have been possible. The techniques worked for me and my circumstances. I hope that they can work for you too.

I listed the rules below in their shortened version under each of the three categories. Each rule corresponds to each chapter, so I used the chapters and rules interchangeably throughout the book. I developed some acronyms to help you recall the rules. Many of the examples that I share in this book are related to law school. I request that as you read them to think of an equivalent scenario related to your field of study. I recommend you read the rules in the order of how they are structured in this book. However, if you want to jump straight to the actual techniques and strategies, you can start with Category II, Rules 5 to 8. These four chapters alone, if implemented diligently, are enough to give you excellent results.

Category I   Preparation rules (**PPPF**)

        Rule 1   Know your **purpose**

        Rule 2   Set your **parameters** or constraints

        Rule 3   Look after your **physical and mental health**

        Rule 4   Have **faith**

Category II   Effective strategies **(GPST)**

Rule 5   Use **graphs, charts, diagrams, pictures and checklists**

Rule 6   **Practice previous years' assessment questions**

Rule 7   **Start early** and plan completion of assessments

Rule 8   **Time management**

Category III   Memory enhancers **(SESI)**

Rule 9   Use **sticky notes and page markers**

Rule 10   **Explain** what you learned to someone

Rule 11   Create a **story**

Rule 12   Use **index or flash cards** for keywords and phrases

My experiences in attaining degrees, learning instruments, writing books, starting businesses and travelling made me realise that I love learning new things. Sometimes those things that we used to hate in the past are the very ones that we might end up loving. You just need to give it a try. Before I wrote my first book, I always wondered how authors find time to put their ideas together and to write them into a book. In my mind, it was almost an impossible task. I had no idea because I have never done it before. The more I thought about it, the more I got curious. When I started looking into how to write a book, I realised that there are techniques and strategies that I could use to overcome the initial mental hurdle about writing a book, so I decided to write my first book. I even managed to complete the book sooner than expected. When I finally sent the manuscript to the publisher, I thought I could do this again. I just needed another idea. Three years later, my second book was published.

Learning is important to our development and growth. It is also important to employ techniques that improve and accelerate our learning process. By doing this, we can retain more information, apply what we learned and even continue to learn more things. Some people asked me whether or not I really had to become a lawyer after becoming an accountant. They never understood my love for learning.

I hope that you will find this book helpful with all the techniques that I share with you and I wish you all the success in your learning.

PREPARATION
RULES

RULE 1: KNOW YOUR **PURPOSE**

It's important to know the reason why you do what you do. Your actions become meaningful and it is easier to get motivated. It's the same when you decide to pursue a course or a degree. The quality of your 'why' determines the amount of focus and effort you will put in and the sacrifices you are willing to make. The 'why' is not necessarily about your ultimate purpose in life. That in itself is a completely different topic. So, you don't need to be overly dramatic at this stage. The key is just to have a strong enough reason why you decided to take the course. The objective of this rule is to build a strong foundation, a starting point on which to focus your energy. Ideally, your reason would be medium or long-term. Below are some examples that you can modify to suit your situation:

1. I want to become a lawyer and help the disadvantaged in my community.
2. I want to become a volunteer lawyer at Legal Aid and help those who cannot afford legal representation.
3. I want to become a doctor so I can help the sick children in Southeast Asia.
4. I want to become a doctor to prove to my teacher that I can amount to something.
5. I want to become a licensed real estate agent.

Notice that these examples of purpose are desires to become someone or something. In order to achieve one of these purposes, you need to make some initial steps. You do this by setting goals. These goals range from short to medium-term. Some examples are:

1. Get into a reputable law firm after completing the law degree in 2024.

2. Become the most outstanding student in the last year of medical school in 2027.
3. Have an overall weighted average of 80% at the completion of the accounting degree.
4. Become the recipient of a prestigious scholarship in the second year of university.
5. Get my real estate agent license in three years.

Notice that these examples of goals have a unit of measure such as grade and time. Notice also that these are not overly dramatic goals like inventing a new hybrid or electric car or inventing a drug to cure cancer. They're simple and attainable. They're also specific and realistic. They are not too far into the future. Avoid setting broad goals like being a good student. Those goals will not get you anywhere because you cannot measure them. It would be difficult or impossible to keep track of your progress. Pick goals that can be achieved in the near future and are also specific enough to act on and make progress towards. You will see that there's a lot of steps involved in achieving a seemingly simple goal. Let's take the first example. Getting into a reputable firm can be achieved by getting good marks to send to prospective employers. Getting good marks may require you to decrease socialising and increase study time. Contacting reputable firms may require getting in contact with the right person at the firm. You may want to get the contact information of the Human Resources Manager that you met at a Career Fair event. Also, you don't just send your university results a year after you met the manager. You may remember the manager, but the manager may not remember you. You start communicating with the manager shortly after the first meeting. Then, maintain regular communication. Once your results are released, you send them together with your other exceptional credentials to the manager. By then, you would have already established rapport and reputation as an exceptional candidate to join the law firm. You can see that just by setting a goal from the beginning, you set things in motion. It gets you to act. It's the first step in achieving your goal. It also sets yourself up to become a great candidate for a graduate position.

Now, let me just briefly talk about life purpose in general so you can compare and contrast it with the purpose I'm talking about when deciding to take a course, by giving you an example. Steve Jobs discovered his calling early in life and revolutionised the whole computer industry. There were a lot of successes and there were also failures, but he persisted. He knew what kinds of things he needed to pursue to stay within the overall life purpose. This is the deductive way of finding your purpose. Today, Apple Inc is one of the world's most valuable companies. Not everyone is fortunate enough to find their life purpose at a young age. However, if you set your mind to it, you are likely to find it sooner rather than later. That's why purpose is very important and good place to start is the career or course you're taking. Find a reason that is strong or deep enough that you don't easily get discouraged when you experience difficulties. You don't want to give up after just one obstacle. Eventually, if you stay long enough, you will find your higher purpose. This is the inductive way of finding your purpose.

Purpose creates focus and focus increases your chances of success. Just be careful where you base your purpose on. Say you've finished high school and you've just received your Australian Tertiary Admission Rank (ATAR) result. Just because you achieved a high ATAR score does not mean you need to get into medicine or law. If your heart is not into something, you will eventually get out of it, physically or mentally. If you stay, you might end up resentful. So, it is better to spend some time now to examine your interests and the things that you think you would like to pursue. Recall your childhood dreams. Ask your mum or dad what you used to tell them what you would want to be when you grow up. Then decide on the purpose. Consider relevant factors but don't solely base your decision on some external metric that's not from your heart like the ATAR score.

Sometimes we don't know exactly what we want to do in life until later in life when we have more experiences. Although it is a lot better to know your purpose early in life, not everyone has that luxury. It may take a few years, decades or two or three careers to finally realise what you're meant to do. Remember that your purpose is based on your own timeline, not on someone else's.

Some of us go through a journey through which we recognise our strengths and weaknesses. They help us realise what we want to pursue for the rest of our lives. In saying that, you don't necessarily need to gain a lot of experience to know your purpose. The key is just to pick one, set it and work towards it. You can change it later when you have more information or when it becomes clearer on which path you want to take.

If you study just for the sake of studying or because there is an examination, that may not be compelling enough to push you to the point where you're willing to make sacrifices. On the other hand, if you set out to be the highest achiever for a particular subject because it's part of your plan to graduate with honours, it's most likely that you will make sacrifices and prioritise studying above everything else.

During the course of your degree, you may start to question and wonder whether it is worth all the time and money, not just about pursuing your degree but also undertaking other endeavours you may have. I did not have a shortage of this feeling. I have been through a lot of failed projects and businesses that planning and starting the next one was a struggle. Somehow, I managed to keep going. I make it a point to at least finish a project that I start so I can at least see the results. Then I decide whether or not to continue or start a new project altogether. At the back of my mind, I still think about my purpose and that gives me enough motivation.

Now, let's talk more about motivation. Some people get motivated by proving the naysayers wrong. For example, the American entrepreneur

Gary Vaynerchuk, more famously known on the internet as Gary V, is motivated by people who hurl criticisms and negative comments at him. This gives him all the more impetus to prove them wrong. A simple search on YouTube about Gary V would bring up a lot of video clips about how he gets motivated when people try to put him down. It's a similar case with Arnold Schwarzenegger where people doubted his dream to become the best bodybuilder. He proved them wrong. He became one of the best if not the best bodybuilder of all time. He also won Mr Universe as well as Mr Olympia multiple times. Later on, he became a Hollywood action film icon. He also became the governor of California.

You can try this little exercise and see if this approach works for you. Make a list of people who put you down, talked down on you and told you that you're not going to amount to anything. If possible, print or write their full names on an A3 size paper and stick it on your wall or door where you can see it every day.

Overall, whether you use a positive motivation where you use strong and positive words to push you to do some action or proving your naysayers wrong like Gary V, the key is to use the approach that gives you enough motivation to act. Use the one that will propel you to take immediate action. Just keep in mind that all these different ways to motivate you are secondary. Your primary motivation should be your purpose.

For a detailed discussion about purpose and how to find it, search Myles Munroe on YouTube. I heard him talk about human potential and purpose at a conference in Melbourne, Australia. I was so inspired that that I immediately bought his book about maximising potential. I then started to watch many of his talks and speeches online about purpose.

RULE 2: SET YOUR **PARAMETERS** OR CONSTRAINTS

I was working full-time when I started law school. I hesitated at first whether work and study would go together. Looking back, I am glad that I did it. If I listened to those who said that it would be impossible to do it, I wouldn't be a lawyer today. That decision to take up law turned out to be one of my best life decisions. Not just because I am now a lawyer but also because it taught me to focus on important things that matter.

The first parameter that I want to discuss is time. For example, because I only have set amount of time allocated to study, I had to force myself to focus on the important topics that are examinable. It helped me to train myself to channel my energy into studying topics that have a direct effect on my final results. I am thankful for this because in my previous degree, there were instances when I liked the subject and I would read the whole textbook including topics that are not relevant to the assessments. Then towards the examination period, I would run out of time and would cram before the examination because I didn't spend enough time mastering the topics that were examinable. Fortunately, I still managed to get good marks. That's why having to study while working gave a structure to my week and helped me establish a routine that forced me to concentrate on tasks that have direct impact on the results I was aiming for. I also found out that daily and weekly routines help maintain our bodies' circadian rhythm that helps regulate our physical and mental well-being. On top of that, I had a constant and reliable source of income to fund my studies and living expenses. So, you can see that by setting the parameters on my limited resource, which is time, I was able to control the activities and ultimately the results that I was aiming for. If you don't do this, you will end up running out of time during examination period like what happened to me a few times in my previous degree.

There are always constraints every time you undertake a project. It is best to identify then categorise them, so you are able to manage them efficiently. For example, money is a big part of going to university that it can almost affect your success or failure. Why? Because you need money to pay your rent, buy textbooks, print out study materials, pay for food and clothing. The list goes on. Money is part of financial constraints or parameters that must be addressed before the semester starts. Part of setting your financial parameters is to set a budget broken down into monthly and weekly amounts. You set the amounts to control them. By doing this activity early on, you can start thinking about possible sources of income and also ways to cut your expenses. The money requirement of being a student seems like a paradox because you go to university to get a degree which you need to get a job to earn money, but you actually need money to help you get started with your degree. Either way, financial constraints are a major part of your success as a student and you don't want to leave them to chance. Define them. Set them. Control them.

Another parameter that must be addressed is logistics. This includes knowing your local community including shops, libraries and recreation facilities. It is helpful to know the type of services they offer and their business hours, so you know when and where to access them. Also, university orientation weeks are a great way to find out about different services offered to students. For example, most universities offer free medical checks and counselling to students. You may not need them right now, but you never know when you will need them. Knowing these things before you start your studies sets you up for your first year of university. You want to get the housekeeping and general information out of the way as much as you can. Prioritise the ones that relate to your health and personal hygiene. They include the doctors, hospitals, chemists or pharmacies. You will also need to know about your local supermarkets, restaurants and their prices so you can create a weekly budget. Plan some occasional dining with friends at reasonably affordable restaurants. It is important to maintain a healthy social life.

You will also need to think about your accommodation while attending university. If you are going to move closer to your university, you may want to consider sharing a house with other students to save money. You may also want to look into using the board and lodging facility or student residence offered by your university. Just keep in mind that this is normally more expensive than sharing a house outside the school premises. Of course, there are other factors that you need to consider in deciding whether to share a house or reside within the university premises. It's not just about saving money but also safety, easy access to university facilities such as libraries and laboratories and social life (meeting other residents and joining indoor and outdoor activities). Pay attention to safety particularly if you frequently use the library or the lab until late at night. Consider the time you will be saving if you reside within the university premises rather than having to drive or commute to the suburbs. Normally, the university residence is an academic yearlong of commitment. Before you sign the contract, you want to know the details of the services being offered. Services such as bed arrangement and whether you will have your own bedroom or sharing with another student. You also want to know how many meals are included, if they are included at all. You want to know the parking facilities for you and your visitors. You also want to know if your friends and family can rent a room or two and if they can get discount by virtue of the fact that you are a university resident.

Another parameter that you need to consider is your lifelines. These are your friends and family or someone that you can call during difficult times. Life is not going to be easy all the time. It is important that you maintain regular communication with your friends and family, even just once a week or twice a month. By doing this, there would be less hesitation to ring them in the future when you need help. You don't need a lot of them otherwise it would be impossible for you to keep up with your studies, your job, your family and friends. You just need to limit it to three or five people that you can trust. You need to set the parameters on the number of people that you need to maintain regular contact with. This is to maintain your sanity and well-being. You can't possibly classify all your Facebook friends as real friends. If you have 150 friends on Facebook, only 10% of that maybe your best friends which is 15. Out of that 15 you may only have 3 or 5 intimate friends that you maintain regular contact with and can call in times of need.

Note that there are also special services both by government and non-for-profit organisations offering help to those who are in distress or suffering from addiction or depression. For example, if you are in Melbourne, Australia and suffering from anxiety or depression, Beyond Blue is always available to take your call on 1300 22 4636. There are a number of non-for-profit organisations that are doing a fantastic job in helping those who are in need. The important point here is that regardless of whether or not you have friends or family that you can rely on in times of need, there is always available help for you. All you need to do is ask.

The last parameter that I want to include in this chapter is your set of skills and assets. You need to take inventory of your skills and assets to date. It could be the fact that you have a very good memory. Perhaps you speak two or three languages. Maybe you play a musical instrument. Your car, your savings and your collection of stamps ranging from the 1850s until 2020. Perhaps you know how to code. One or more of these things could be a potential source of income while you attend university. It could even become a source of inspiration for a business opportunity. That's why it's important to examine what you already possess and make use of them. There's nothing wrong with getting a job with McDonald's or the supermarket, which is what many teenagers do, but sometimes we search for opportunities somewhere else while all this time, that million-dollar idea was trapped inside of you. So, before you start exploring other territories, start with your own backyard first. You will save time, money and effort and you may very well find exactly what you are looking for.

RULE 3: LOOK AFTER YOUR **PHYSICAL AND MENTAL HEALTH**

Physical and mental health should be part of Rule 2 on setting parameters, but it is very important that it warrants a separate chapter. If you are suffering from a disease that affects your ability to study and learn, it will be hard for you to attend university; regardless of how determined you are. That's why it's important to look after your physical and mental well-being. We hear all those advertisements all the time about maintaining a healthy lifestyle, but we still take our health for granted. We never actually do anything to maintain or improve it until we get sick. When we are healthy, we never think about sickness. We just think that we are always going to be healthy. This was certainly the case for me when I was a teenager. I thought I was invincible. Fortunately, I was surrounded with people who encouraged me and taught me the value of exercise and maintaining a good physical health. My uncle used to knock on my door at 5:00 in the morning to go for a jog. We would go for a few laps around the university square. I didn't like it at first because sometimes I would stay up to finish some readings and would go to bed late. That meant I would only have around 5 or 6 hours of sleep, but once the routine was set and became part of my system, getting up at 5:00 in the morning wasn't too bad after all.

Somewhere down the track, I stopped jogging. I got busy. Then someone at the firm I was working at, went to the gym every week. He invited me to join him. So, I did. Pretty soon, going to the gym became part of my weekly routine again. I did that for about a year.

Then I moved to Melbourne and got busy again. No jogging, no gym. Then, some family members started talking about exercise and gym and that there was a discounted gym membership that was available for me. I signed up. I was back in the gym routine again.

I moved to a new suburb and guess what? I got busy again. I stopped going to the gym. I would go for random jogs once in a while, but more often not I would find an excuse not to do it. It felt like there were two voices in me. One voice was telling me to do more jogging; another was telling me to don't even bother.

It is very easy to skip the gym or exercise. We would find even the lamest excuse just to avoid it. If it's cold outside or drizzling, we exaggerate like it was freezing or pouring. We justify our inaction. We do it all the time, including me.

Years later after hearing stories about people I know who developed different kinds of diseases and how their lifestyle is a major contributor, I went back to my daily jogging routine. Nowadays, I jog every morning for about three kilometres to kickstart my day. I started thinking that those friends and family whom we thought are inflicting pain on us are actually trying to make us better. Sometimes our perception is shaped by what we are going through particularly if we are under a lot of stress or pressure. As we mature and as our circumstances change, we look back and realise that what happened to us in the past wasn't too bad after all. In fact, some of them made us stronger and better people.

Anyway, I think one of the main lessons with my story is that the people around us play an important role in how we develop our habits and routines. It is vital that we surround ourselves with people who can empower and encourage us to help maintain our physical as well as mental well-being.

Another very important aspect of our well-being is sleep. For someone who used to have a lot of sleepless nights, I know exactly how it feels when you don't have enough sleep. When I can't sleep the night before, I suffer the next day. Sometimes the sleepless nights can go on for two or three consecutive nights and I don't perform properly at school.

That's why I have to take magnesium tablets that help induce sleep. Sometimes they work, sometimes they don't. I also have to take to zinc tablets that help boost my immune system to compensate the lack of sleep. It sucks when you don't get enough sleep. You get easily annoyed, irritated and impatient. Sometimes you can't get things done properly and you become dissatisfied. You go into this vicious cycle of sleep deprivation and decreased productivity. There are a lot of resources online about how to get a good sleep but if your sleeplessness is getting out of control, see a doctor or a sleep specialist.

Now, let's talk about downtime and study breaks. It is important to allow for some downtime where you absolutely don't do any study. You incorporate breaks into your daily and weekly schedules. Downtime can vary from a few minutes to a few days. I used to have a rule for myself that every time I felt the slightest tiredness and just about to reach a point where I couldn't absorb any more information, I would stop from whatever I was doing and would force myself to have an early lunch or dinner; go to bed; or go for a walk. It's also a good idea to have a break every hour or so when you are reading or writing your assignments. Exercise not just your body and limbs but also your eyes. One of the reasons I developed short-sightedness was because I wasn't taking enough breaks away from my desk and computer. It's not healthy to be in front of the screen all the time. You're meant to look outside your window and away from your computer once in a while. You need to strike a balance on what you look at between short-distances and long-distances. It was too late for me because by the time I went to the optometrist and told me all these things, damage was already done to my eyes. I didn't have a choice but to get prescription glasses. I didn't only have issues with my eyes. I also developed back issues for sitting too long without regular breaks. I had to see an osteopath to fix me.

That's why it is very important to seek professional advice early on about health, posture and well-being in general. There might be things or habits that you developed all these years that may have adverse impact on your well-being. Many of these professionals have their own YouTube channels so it's probably best to start with their videos and then book an appointment if you need to.

Let me give you some more tips about study breaks. I would take breaks when I can no longer absorb what I'm reading. This would be around after 20 or 30 minutes of focused reading. There is no point jamming more information in your head if it there is no more room for it. It is much better to take a proper break like watch a movie, go for a run or have an early lunch. You will notice that your productivity goes up again when you resume your study session. The idea behind doing activities during study breaks is to release endorphins in your bloodstream. Endorphins are hormones that can inhibit pain and produce euphoria. Some people use apps like Pomodoro which reminds you to take a break after 20 or 25 minutes. Although I'm not totally opposed to it, I believe that this may not be the optimal way of doing study breaks. The reason is that you don't want to interrupt the flow or continuity of thought while you are reading an important concept or argument just because the 20-minute reminder is up. Sometimes, it can take an hour to understand a very complex topic; or 15 minutes to digest a very interesting concept. You just need to find that length of time that gives you the optimal focus and productivity.

It is also worth knowing what times your body and mind operate effectively. When I study early in the morning my learning absorption rate is a lot faster than if I study in the afternoon or after work. I would say that this is true because in the morning after a good sleep, our cells would have just been replenished. As the day progresses, our productivity goes down. That's why if I want to have a lot done for the day, I try to do as much as I can in the first five hours of the day.

Now, let's talk about technology and gadgets. Try to set your laptop or phone brightness so it is not too bright for your eyes. You can do this on your iPhone so that the recommended brightness is set depending on the time of the day. Also, when you're doing late night studying, use 'night shift mode' to minimise the amount of blue light to help you fall asleep faster. Also, try to reduce your exposure to electronic gadgets. For example, I used to keep my smartphone beside my bed and it wasn't a good idea. I would sometimes hear notifications in the middle of the night, and it was disrupting my already broken sleep. Then later on I started leaving my phone in the living room to charge overnight. It made a lot of difference. There was no more temptation to check the notifications and scrolling for updates and news feeds. It was definitely a step forward.

Another important aspect of well-being is diet. You need to watch what you eat. Look into various food products that boost your immune system and not just those that make you lose weight. Remember that if you don't have a strong immune system, it will make you vulnerable to illnesses. When you are sick, it will put you behind schedule because you will not be able to attend classes, do your assignment and prepare for examinations. You will also need time to recover. Hydrate yourself properly by drinking plenty of water every day.

Physical and mental well-being is affected by other factors like financial constraints discussed in Chapter 2. Many of the healthy food and drink products these days are getting more expensive and they have to be taken into account when you create your weekly budget. However, if you are resourceful enough, you can find out good deals and bargain at Asian supermarkets and shops. Just do some research about your local shops and you'll see that there are a number of Asian places that sell healthy products at affordable prices.

Overall, just remember that no amount of study techniques and strategies can replace a good health.

RULE 4: HAVE FAITH

This rule is probably the most important part of my life as a lifelong learner. It helped me a lot at law school precisely because it's something but law. I already had enough consumption of legislation printouts, law handbooks, law textbooks and notes about legal concepts. I needed something more ethereal. I know that faith is probably the last thing that a law student would think about, or any other student for that matter. It has questions about our purpose: who we are; where we came from; and where we are going to. Law uses reason to formulate arguments. Faith is not necessarily approached the same way. In fact, it is the opposite in many instances. Even so, it was particularly helpful for me when things happened in my life that I could not logically explain. It wasn't about how well I referenced legal sources for my assignments or how quickly I cited authorities on religious freedom. Faith goes to the core of your being. Perhaps, the means to test your inner strength. It was for me—a strength that is closely related to the reason why I decided to go to law school in the first place. The more I examined my faith, the stronger I believed that it's closely linked to my mental well-being. When you have a strong foundation on what your beliefs are and if they are grounded on sound historical and philosophical underpinnings, you are better equipped to face difficulties and pain because you have the lens through which you can perceive events.

Let me give you this scenario. There were students that I read about from other universities, both in Australia and overseas, who committed suicide. Their reasons for hurting themselves vary and we're not going to talk about those in this book. I am not an expert in this area, nor I purport to sound like one. I am just sharing how I tackled my own issues when I was at my lowest point in my life which was during my time at law school. I would be exposing some of my vulnerability here but if this means potentially helping you find your inner strength, then so be it. Please bear with me as I share you this part of my life.

It was during the second half of 2017 and it's only been a few weeks after the trimester started. Spring has just started, and it was my second year of law school. The subjects were getting difficult. Studies demanded more of my time and I was working full-time. I had to adjust my schedule to somehow free up some more time to study. I had to do more research, readings and analyses. I felt like my head was going to burst. On top of this, I was also helping a family friend with their business accounting needs. There was just too much on my plate. I was so overwhelmed with all the things and commitments that I had at that time. I then started to wonder if there was something wrong with me. It got to a point where I started to question the validity of my own existence. I thought about the worst things. I was visualising a painful life with too much burden and no hope. It was difficult, very difficult. There were instances when someone would talk to me and I would go blank all of a sudden. A person would talk about a topic that I would be interested in and we would engage in a good conversation. Then some negative thoughts would suddenly creep into my mind and I would miss some parts of the conversation. I became frustrated. It was an endless cycle of negative thoughts that produced negative emotions and I could not get out. I was on the verge of calling it quits (end it all) when I decided to visit my older brother. I haven't visited him for a while, so it made me feel a little bit better because it was something to look forward to. It was painful at first but it got better as I kept driving. When I got to his place, I told him about what I was going through. We had a good and deep conversation that night. It was one of the most meaningful conversations I had in a long time. He gave me a lot of advice. He said that we all go through pain for a reason. He said that in the end, it is not really about us. It's about what we do to glorify the Creator. I went to bed with that thought. I got up the next day, still thinking about what my brother said. Then I drove to university to study for the upcoming examinations. I decided to go for a walk that morning at university, before doing any study. I felt some relief every time I thought about what my brother said the night before. Knowing that there is someone out there, bigger and greater than me, who is in control, gives me a sense of hope that everything will be fine. While I was walking, I admired the beauty of the lilies and the sound of the birds that chirped 'good morning.' I smelled the fragrance of the flowers. The sunshine on my shoulders made me happy. I began to appreciate these little things in nature again. I could not even remember the last time I did that. On the last part of my walk, I decided from that moment on, I would dedicate all my projects to my Creator, instead of myself. The glory and praises belong to the Creator, not me. I spent too much time thinking about me, my work and my studies that I neglected my own spirituality, my own existence.

From the lowest point of my life, emerging from that pit and appreciating the beauty of life would not have been possible without the people around me and the faith that I developed over the years. That's why it's important that you have at least some people in your life whom you trust that you know you can talk to about anything. They could be a member of your family or a close friend. In a western society where we prefer figuring things out ourselves, sometimes it is difficult to reach out to other people for help. We don't realise that our friends and family are more than willing to help if we just reach out to them. We just need to make the first move and ask for help.

This whole experience made me realise one very important thing–that I am just a vessel of someone or something bigger than myself. That person could be God. That something could be your purpose. Since I am just a vessel, the main cargo is more important. Just remember that purpose is normally long-term, something that goes beyond finish lines and awards. It's oriented towards helping others. It is not to finish law school or to be the best lawyer in town. Going to university is just the first step towards a greater purpose.

We don't know exactly what the future holds. No matter how certain we feel that the path that we are treading on now is the right one, there's no guarantee that it would be the same path we will end up with. Assure yourself that whatever happens with your university results or marks, that they will all work out for good in the overall scheme of things. Even if the final results turn out to be a failure, you will gain valuable lessons from the whole experience. In fact, the lessons that we learn from failures and pain are more powerful than the things we learn from our successes.

I'll end this chapter with a realisation about my life and journey. While writing this book, I recalled some life-threatening moments in my life but somehow there was always a divine intervention that kept me well and alive all this time.

The first one was when I was crossing a two-way road, jaywalking actually. I checked both directions for approaching cars. For some reason, I must have underestimated the speed of the approaching bus from the other direction because halfway through in the middle of the road, the bus was already a few metres away from me. I was going to run across all the way to the other side of the road but something stopped me right on the white line marking that divided the road and cars from both directions.

The second one was when I was mugged by three men while I was walking back home from the library to study for the examination the next day. I didn't know if they had weapons. I was forced to the ground with my face down while they took my bag. The bag had all the study materials I needed for the examination. I suffered some bruises, but they were nothing compared to the trauma that left me shocked and sleepless until the next day when I took the examination. That morning before the examination, I received a call from the police that they found my bag. I never thought that I would see my bag again. When I got to the police station and opened my bag, all my study materials were still there, the things I needed for the examination. The only thing that was missing was my spare old mobile phone which I wasn't too worried about.

These events remind me that I still have a reason to live and a purpose to fulfill.

EFFECTIVE STRATEGIES

RULE 5: USE: **USE GRAPHS, CHARTS, DIAGRAMS, PICTURES AND CHECKLISTS**

Graphs, charts, diagrams, pictures and checklists are tools to enhance comprehension. They also facilitate analysis and interpretation of relevant information. They helped me understand complex concepts using less or no words at all. Often, I would spend a few minutes looking at the diagram and I can pick-up what the author is trying to say. There are times when I would read a chapter about a topic for an hour and l would only have a vague idea of the message the writer is trying to convey.

Graphs and charts are generally used to show trends or patterns over a period of time. You would rather look at the graph of Melbourne coffee consumption for example over a period of 15 years than reading a page of text about it with a year-by-year breakdown. You would rather use a chart in your class or sales presentation about the level of sales achieved during the year broken down into quarters. You'll be able to also see in visual terms the relationship of each quarter achievement in relation or comparison to other quarters and the year as a whole.

There are instances when diagrams are the best way to illustrate a point. They are also a very effective tool in showing a connection of different concepts.

Pictures are used for word and concept associations. You create a diagram of concepts with an image in the middle to represent the connection that they're all from the same topic. During review time, you just recall that image all the related concepts will come alive in your mind.

Checklists are a great tool to ensure that you don't miss anything. They're particularly helpful when you're trying to learn a process or a new skill that involves a number of steps to get to a competent level. Even professionals such as pilots and surgeons use checklists to ensure they don't miss anything.

Another tool that you may already know is mind mapping. If you want to know more about it, look up Tony Buzan. He is the one who popularised the mind mapping concept and probably the best person to explain how to use it effectively. He explained the process of starting with an image in the middle of the diagram because it stimulates memory. You then create branches from that central image and then sub-branches for up to any number of sub-levels you desire. The use of diagrams is in and of itself an old method that is still proven to be effective. The types of diagrams and the way they are constructed may have evolved into coloured and animated versions these days, but the rationale behind their use is still the same—easy and quick comprehension of an idea.

I use diagrams to plan as well as track my progress of a project or a topic if I'm studying. I also used diagrams to summarise concepts that I learned from cases and sections of a legislation. Diagrams are useful to show hierarchies of courts and case authorities or precedents.

Overall, graphs, charts, diagrams, pictures and checklists are a great way not just to prepare for assessments and examinations but also in learning a new skill or field. Below are some examples to show you how certain information is understood better when presented in a particular format. Fictitious data are used for the graph and the chart.

Graph

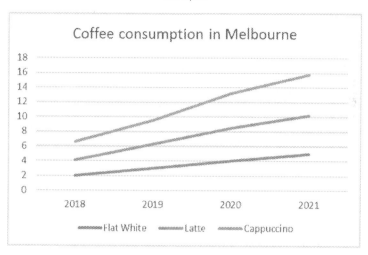

Chart

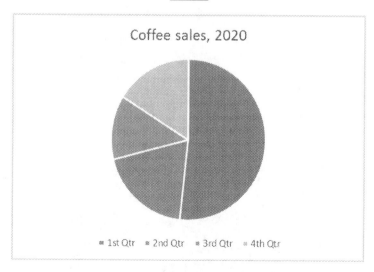

Diagram

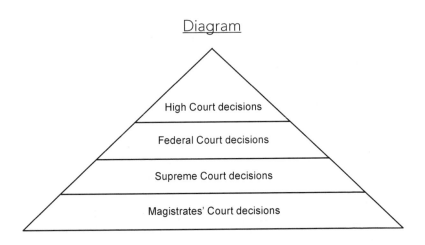

High Court decisions

Federal Court decisions

Supreme Court decisions

Magistrates' Court decisions

Picture

Photo by Toa Heftiba on Unsplash

Checklist

International travel checklist:

1. Cities or countries to visit ☐
2. Visa requirements of the cities or countries ☐
3. Travel advisory or warnings about those cities or countries ☐
4. Final list of cities to visit ☐
5. Requirements other than visa such as medical insurance ☐
6. Customs and quarantine requirements of each country ☐
7. Unexpired passport (6 to 12 months before expiry) ☐
8. Travel insurance ☐
9. Activities covered by the insurance ☐
10. Currency used for each city ☐
11. Need to purchase currency before departure? ☐
12. Travel money or card ☐
13. Emergency contact numbers in each city ☐
14. Emergency contact information back home ☐
15. Photocopies of visas and passport in bags and luggage ☐
16. Phone and spare phone ☐
17. Debit cards and spare debit cards ☐
18. Charger and power banks ☐
19. Medications ☐
20. Tickets ready? ☐
21. Muesli bars ☐
22. Accommodation organised ☐
23. Transportation organised ☐
24. Automatic payment organised for bills while away ☐
25. People who will look after house and car while away ☐
26. Camera and spare camera ☐
27. Enough jackets, jeans, shirts, socks and underwear ☐
28. Transportation to the airport ☐

RULE 6: PRACTICE PREVIOUS YEARS' ASSESSMENT QUESTIONS

Based on my experience, this is, I would say, the most important out of the effective strategies and probably out of the 12 rules other than Rule 4 about faith. Let me explain.

Before I discovered this technique, I would buy and start reading the textbook for a particular subject even before the semester starts. I would also go through the topic outline diligently once they are released at the start of the semester. I read. I studied. At the end of the semester when I sat for the examination and read the first question, I could not write anything for a few minutes. Not because I didn't know about the question but because I was running a few scenarios in my head on how to answer the question and I didn't know which one to pick. Although I had the ideas and concepts in my head, I could not think of an efficient way of structuring my thoughts properly that would sufficiently address the question. They were all jumbled up. As a result, I ran out of time towards the end and only wrote a couple of sentences for the remaining two questions. I had completely no idea of what the examination questions would look like and how they were formulated in a final examination scenario. I still managed to pass the examination and earned a C (credit) for the subject. It would have been a completely different scenario if I learned about this technique early on my student life.

I may have understood the topics and concepts very well but that's not how I was assessed and marked. I was examined on how well I applied those concepts to resolve cases and problems. So, you need to learn how to do this process well—application of concepts and principles to solve problems. You won't have time to do this during examination. You need to start to practise what you learn during the semester as early as you can by attempting previous years' examinations.

Practising previous examination questions will help gauge your understanding of the topics. It will also force you to recall what you have learned so far during the semester and whether or not you will need to exert more effort and spend more time studying. Answering previous examinations is far more effective than reading the topic materials or textbook multiple times.

There are a number of ways on how you want to do this activity. For example, you can set up a pretend examination in your bedroom as if you're at the examination venue. You set the timer on and make sure you stop writing when the time is up. This will help you gauge how much work you still need to do, to confidently answer possible examination questions. You will also develop your own structure for your answers. You may start with a conclusion and then support it with arguments, or you may want to start with facts, data or arguments to build to a conclusion. For example, at law school, there is a method called IRAC in answering questions. It stands for Issue, Rule, Analysis, Conclusion. Students need to identify what the issues are (issue); then cite the relevant law needed to solve the issues (rule); analyse the issues using the law which involves applying the legal principles to the issues at hand (analysis); and conclude with scenarios of what the possible outcomes are (conclusion). The more questions you attempt to answer, the more confident you will get in answering examination questions. The questions in the actual examination may not necessarily be the same as your practice ones but you will have a fairly good idea on how the questions are formulated. It won't be a complete surprise to you when you sit the actual examination.

Another piece of information that you need to know about examinations is that many subjects at university have allocated at least 50% for the final examination as part of your overall grade. Ensure that you exert at least 50% of your time and efforts for that examination. Be mindful of the different components for the assessments because you don't want to spend majority of your time on something that is only worth 10% out of the total grade.

Another way of doing practice questions is to just attempt one or two questions at a time as you progress through the semester. Some of the questions may not make sense to you early on during the semester as they may not have been discussed yet in class, but you can certainly read ahead. Nothing stops you from studying ahead of the schedule so you can start answering the questions on the practice examinations. You don't necessarily need to read all the materials. You just go to the specific pages of the textbook or materials where you can find the concepts and principles you need to answer the practice questions. This is targeted learning. You search for the relevant principles that will help you answer the practice questions. This is the key—knowing the key principles in each topic. That's what you're going to be assessed on, the principles, not on data or facts. Well, it was in my case at least. I didn't necessarily have to follow the subject outline in order. You need to control your own learning process. Consider the subject outline as a guide rather than a gospel. Later on, when you start discussing that topic in class, those things that you read in advance will become clearer.

When answering the practice questions, try to put your answers in a word file so you can edit and refine them later on. You will find that as you progress through the semester and review the practice questions, the quality of your answers will improve. Towards the end of the teaching period, you can print these answers as part of your revision or review. During law school, I used to categorise the practice questions based on topics on the subject outline. For constitutional law for example, I would have a group of questions and answers relating to freedom of religion, say three pages' worth; another group of questions and answers relating to trade between states; another group for national security; and the list goes on. I would make an 18-font-sized and bold type heading for each group or category so it would be easier for me to look for it in an open-book examination. There will be instances where the questions in the actual examinations are very similar if not the same with the ones that you have practised on and all you need to do is copy the answers that you have prepared to your examination booklet.

Many examinations in undergraduate studies test your understanding of the current mainstream principles in your field. Teachers don't always include old, alternative or peripheral concepts unless they are necessary for comparison and contrast. If you do happen to read or study these concepts, try not to spend too long on them unless you really have a lot of time to spare. Time is critical during revision or review time and you want to spend majority of it in topics and principles that are most likely to be examinable.

Now, the only thing left to think about is where to get these practice examination questions. During my time at law school, many lecturers made the previous examination papers available to all students early on the semester. Some teachers uploaded them during the revision period at the end of the teaching period. Sometimes these examination papers are also available in the library for download, so check with your librarian where you can get past years' examination papers. You can also ask other students who have taken the subject before and if they can recall some of the questions. There are also other resources available from student websites like www.studentvip. com.au for those who are studying in Australia. They are an excellent source of notes, cheap textbooks and tutors. It also has campus maps of many universities that can help navigate around campus. It has an app version of the map so you can download it from the App Store or Google play.

Anyway, I just want to reiterate that in my opinion, this is the most important technique that I found as a student that will actually help in improving examination results. It was particularly helpful for me as a law student while I was also working full-time. Start practising answering examination questions early in the semester and it will certainly improve the way you structure your answers and how you manage your time when you sit the actual examinations. It will also help you channel your energy and time more efficiently to important topics and principles that are examinable. You don't want to do what I did–get distracted with commentaries, other topics and 'did you know?' sections of the textbooks. It's alright if you're reading the books for leisure but not if you're preparing for assessments. Remember, the goal here is to achieve good or excellent marks and not to be entertained by interesting facts and figures.

Control your reading, focus your effort, channel your energy and concentrate all your learning time on targeted topics and principles. Answer past years' examination papers.

RULE 7: START EARLY AND PLAN COMPLETION OF DEGREE AND ASSESSMENTS

Planning is involved in various stages of your university life. You can create either a high-level planning or a detailed planning. You can even break down the detailed planning further into different time categories such as monthly, weekly, daily and hourly routines.

1. Your whole degree broken down into semesters and summer breaks.
2. Semesters and summer breaks broken down into weeks.
3. Weekly goals broken down into daily tasks.
4. Daily tasks broken down into hourly routines.

Doing this exercise will give you a bird's eye view of what the whole course structure looks like and when certain subjects can be taken. Some subjects have pre-requisite units before you can take them. So, ensure that you have the right order of the subjects in each semester. You don't want to be in a situation where you can't enrol for a particular subject in semester 2 this year because you haven't taken the pre-requisite subject that is only offered in semester 1. You will have to wait until next year when semester 1 starts again. You'll end up taking that particular subject in semester 2 next year and you'll be delayed for a year just for that. I recommend that you take the time to plan your degree and break it down by semesters including summer breaks, if you plan to take a subject or two during the summer period. Consider the following scenarios.

First scenario
You decided to get away for the weekend to Geelong which is about an hour drive from Melbourne. It was Saturday morning, and you rang some places for overnight accommodation. No

vacancies. You were disappointed. You decided to go anyway. You were thinking to look for accommodation once you get there and if there is still no vacancy that you would just drive home that night. Before you started the car, you remembered that you needed to finish some reports for a presentation on Monday. You went back inside the house to grab your laptop and by the time you were ready to leave, it was already past lunchtime. You drove to Geelong. You walked around the area and checked out some shops. After a few minutes, you got hungry. You didn't have breakfast because you were busy ringing places for an overnight stay. You found a café nearby and so you stopped by to have a late lunch there instead of walking further towards the waterfront. By the time you finished your lunch it was starting to get dark, so you hurried to get a glimpse of the waterfront area. You had a quick look of the beach and also found a nice restaurant overlooking the beach. You wished you had your lunch there. You looked at your watch, it was 18:25. You thought it wasn't worth checking for any accommodation at that time of the night, so you decided to drive back home.

Second scenario
You decided to have a weekend getaway in Geelong, and you wanted to stay there for a couple of days. You checked with your manager at work if you could take next Friday off. Your leave was approved. You searched on Airbnb and you found a nice accommodation. You booked and paid for it. You did some research and found a very good brunch place with great reviews. You booked a brunch at 11 am. You also found a 4.5-star restaurant. You booked dinner at 7 pm. You allocated the next day to explore the area including the waterfront. You planned to have breakfast on Sunday morning before driving home. You had a fantastic weekend. You were back at work on Monday feeling refreshed.

Analysis

The second scenario is obviously the better one. It is better because the whole purpose of going for a weekend getaway is pleasure and we can see from the facts that the purpose was achieved. Notice that the initial steps of applying for leave, researching and booking the accommodation, brunch and dinner were not totally a very exciting experience. It took a bit of work. Despite all these, we still consider the second scenario as a better one not based on the initial steps taken but based on the outcome. The purpose of a weekend getaway is to relax and have a good time and that purpose was clearly achieved.

Notice in the second scenario that having a plan and a schedule of activities as well as commitments with other people (accommodation and food places), increases the probability of doing to them. You'll also end up optimising and maximising your time. If you don't have a plan at all, you have nothing to commit to in the first place, so start something, even if it's just a simple diagram about what you want to do. Don't go into the minute details at the start. That will come naturally later on when you start doing some action and as you think through your diagram. In the past, when I started thinking about the detailed steps of something I wanted to do, my mind started to shut off. Then I would go do something else. Our brains are designed to avoid pain. Detailed steps are pain. So, unless you are really disciplined, don't start with the detailed steps of something you want to do.

My example

I wanted to know when exactly when I could complete my degree. I was (and still am) working full-time so I needed to know exactly what subjects I'd be taking each semester, so I don't take the difficult subjects during the end of financial year period as well as calendar year when it's busy at work. I also made sure to take subjects in the order recommended by the course planner to meet the pre-requisite conditions of the course. I had to regularly contact the course coordinator who was helping me plan my degree. We came up with a course planner broken down into years and semesters. I would review the course planner every six months for adjustments like dropping a subject from semester two and taking a summer elective subject instead because it was busy at work during semester two. There was one semester where I took four subjects (full-time load) while working full-time. This was possible because I already had some knowledge about two of the elective subjects. Since there were changes to my course planner every semester, I was constantly updating it at the end of the semester when I receive the results.

I would also have a weekly schedule that incorporates my routines such as jogging, reviewing notes, shopping, YouTube and catching-up with friends. You can download a template of this weekly schedule from www.lifeofavessel.com.

One of the advantages of having worked out your degree early on is you can start learning about the subjects even before the semester starts. I used to search YouTube videos about subjects like criminal law and constitutional law just to gauge how difficult the subjects are. The videos turned out to be interesting and entertaining and I ended up watching a whole bunch about those subjects, way before the semester started.

Planning can be broken down into sub-topics or sub-principles depending on the complexity of your subject. For example, I would make a checklist of the main rules, concepts and principles that we were meant to learn for a particular subject. I would then include exceptions, sub-concepts, sub-principles. I made sure that I study the main rules and principles first concepts. Once the main principles are done, I would study the exceptions and sub-principles. It's important to distinguish the main rule or principles from the exceptions.

For example, in criminal law the rule in double jeopardy is that once someone is convicted or acquitted of an offence, a person can't be tried again for the same offence. There are exceptions to this main rule depending on which jurisdiction. If this is in Victoria, exceptions are contained in the legislation. Some of the exceptions include cases where the person is charged and convicted of a lesser offence arising out of the same circumstances; or when the Director of Public Prosecutions applies to the Court of Appeal for an order to set aside previous acquittal before proceeding to prosecute because of fresh and compelling evidence. Anyway, this example may not make sense to you, but the point is to master the main rules first before studying the exceptions and other principles.

There are other benefits of planning and doing the work early. For example, it allows time for relaxation as the examinations are fast approaching. While others are cramming, you are relaxing. A relaxed mind is in a better position to take the examinations than a sleepless one.

Below are more tips I can give you about different ways to start early during the semester:

1. Go over the subject outline (previous or current semester) and familiarise yourself with the examinable topics.
2. Read comments and tips from previous students.
3. Get a hold of previous students' notes or buy from a student resource service like www.studentvip.com.au. Make your own notes as the semester progresses.
4. Get hold of previous years' examination papers.
5. Buy a second-hand book to read during the summer break.
6. Browse lecture slides first or read the pages on the textbook before attending the lecture.
7. Read the take-home assignment at the start of the semester (so you know what topics to focus on).

8. Learn how to speed-read (there are a lot of YouTube videos about this).

9. Watch YouTube videos about your future subjects.

10. Assess the difficulty level of the subject based on previous students' feedback.

RULE 8: TIME MANAGEMENT

Time management may be considered overrated for those who don't really understand its mechanics and how to implement it effectively. However, time management is not just about fixing your schedule to accomplish all tasks that need to be done. This is about allocating time for things that matter. This rule is very much related to planning in Rule 7 or Chapter 7. When you plan, you need to question whether an entry to your schedule is essential or not. Remember that saving time from not having to do non-essential or non-productive activities will give you more time for essential and productive ones.

There are different approaches to time management. Some of the ideas that I share in this chapter may overlap to some extent with the ones I already explained in Chapter 7.

One approach to time management is to increase speed of learning. You can implement this through listening to audio lectures and reading textbooks. For example, I used to increase the audio lecture speed to either 1.5x or 1.75 depending how slow or fast the lecturer was. Ideally, you would increase the speed to a level that will allow for both comprehension and clarity. There's no point increasing the speed to 2.0x for example because you want to finish the audio lecture quickly, if you can't understand a word from it. I also used a few speed-reading techniques like skimming before reading; reading the blurb and table of contents before reading; using a pen to guide my eyes to speed-read; using my peripheral vision; training my eyes to look at a page like you look at a photo; writing down what I know about the topic; the list goes on.

Another approach to time management is to find unutilised time like reading textbooks or listening to lectures while on the train or bus, driving to work, doing some exercise, taking a shower or having dinner. Let me share to you what happened in my first semester of law school. By the way, that semester was a big one for me because it was an adjustment period—whether I could do both work and study. I enrolled to only two subjects just to see how and what law school was like. At the end of the first semester, I felt like I could handle law school and work at the same time. The following year, I increased my subjects to three for semester one and even earned a D (Distinction) for one of them. As I progressed through law school, my reading speed increased partly because my legal vocabulary increased. I watched and read about different techniques for speed-reading and also came up with my own style from combining different techniques I've learned on YouTube. I was conscious not to get distracted with other things while watching YouTube videos. My goal was to improve my speed-reading skills, so I just focused on extracting information that relate to speed-reading and not get sucked into the marketing and promotion traps. Otherwise, it would defeat the purpose of trying to save or manage time effectively. Know what you want, get it, then move on.

Let me share with you some more strategies that I used at law school relating to saving and managing time.

1. If there is a summary or conclusion of a topic, read it first before anything else. The summary will give you an idea of what the section or chapter is about. It will help you gauge whether or not you need to spend more or less time on the chapter depending on the level of knowledge you may or may not have about a topic. Do not start with the actual chapter, especially if you don't have a good existing knowledge about the topic. It will just unnecessarily consume time that you could be spending on more important chapters.

2. Save time by skipping the blurb, introduction and the table of contents of the textbook. Not all the contents in the textbook will be examinable. Use the unit guide or subject outline

provided by the lecturer. Focus on the chapters indicated on the guide. That's the purpose of the unit guide.

3. Set a maximum time limit for a chapter or topic by writing it down on a post-it or sticky note and put it where it's visible all the time. You may want to finish an easy chapter in 25 minutes or a difficult one in an hour. Then, take a break before going on to the next one. You will be able to quantify your achievement in terms of number of chapters read per day. This activity will also increase the probability that you will finish all the topic readings. Don't worry too much about full comprehension at this stage. As you progress through the semester, your knowledge of the subject will increase. By the time you do semester review, you'll be able to make sense of those sections that you didn't understand the first time around.

4. I used to listen to audio lectures twice. The first round is just pure listening at 2.0x speed as long as it's comprehensible. The second round is taking notes while listening at 1.5x speed.

5. If you run out of time to review for the assessment or examination, pull out the course or subject outline and go through the topics. Write down a paragraph or two about each topic that will encapsulate the main rules and principles. You may include exceptions and other principles but focus on the main ones. You will probably need 30 minutes or an hour for each topic for this activity.

6. Ensure that you check your assessment timetable early and set up reminders using different platforms (Google calendar, iCal, Outlook, Yahoo, etc.) days before the actual date of assessment or examination. Also ensure that you know where the examination venue is and how to get there. Estimate travel time. If you are driving to the venue, check for parking. If you're catching public transport, check the timetable. If all else fails, you can always use an Uber or a cab. Allow for

things like heavy traffic, flat tire, looking for a parking spot, looking for the examination room and bathroom.

7. Skim the chapter before reading it. By doing this, your brain will recall existing knowledge about the topic when you see familiar words and phrases. Once you do the actual reading, your existing knowledge will be confirmed or reinforced and the updated version of that knowledge will be better stored in your memory.

8. If possible, choose a textbook that has two or more authors. I found that they are better written, more understandable and less or no errors. I think the reason is that the other writers are more likely to proof-read the manuscript as they share the authorship with other people. They are also able to provide suggestions to improve the book. A book that you can easily understand in one round of reading will save you time. Errors and poor writing can slow you down. You'll be spending extra time trying to figure what they actually mean without the errors.

9. Make use of the small chunks of time in between activities. For example, while waiting for your train or bus, between classes, or waiting for your doctor's appointment.

10. When I did my exchange at Aarhus University in Denmark, I went to travel throughout Europe and whenever I was on a train, bus or airplane to another city, I was working on my assignment. By the end of my trip and after 13 cities, I finished the assignment and submitted it before I flew back to Australia.

11. Use sticky notes for key words and prompts and put them in strategic places around the house where you see them all the time such as the bedroom and also the bathroom. The words and prompts have corresponding index card versions which include explanation about them. More explanation about sticky notes in Chapter 9 and index cards in Chapter

12. The sooner you use them, the more time you save later on during revision or review time.

12. Convert your car into a classroom by listening to audio lectures. So, whenever you drive to the supermarket or university or go for a weekend getaway, you'll be listening to your audio lectures instead of Dance Monkey or Ariana Grande.

The main idea behind Rule 8 is that you take control of your limited resource—time. Otherwise, you will always end up running out of time and you won't achieve great results. Implement Chapter 8 in conjunction with Chapter 7 and you will see great results. In fact, all the four rules under the effective strategies category, if implemented diligently, are enough to give you excellent results. Remember that it is not about how much resources you have, it's about what you do with the resources you have that counts. This is true for money and other assets, your skills and abilities, accumulated knowledge and people that you know in the industry and other connections.

It's funny that everyone has the same 24 hours in a day and yet the output that people generate from it varies quite a lot. Manage every hour you have.

RULE 9: USE **STICKY NOTES AND PAGE MARKERS**

Most of my examinations at law school were open book—we were allowed to bring any written materials at the examination. This may sound reassuring, but I wasn't completely impressed about it at first. We were only given two hours to complete the examination plus fifteen minutes for reading time. The questions were also harder. In my previous degree, many of the examinations were closed book so we couldn't use any written materials at the examination. For some reason, I preferred this kind of examination because we had more time to answer the questions and they were not as difficult as open book law examinations. I quickly realised that if I were to at least survive law school, I needed to change my mindset of how to prepare for the examination. Instead of doing a lot of memory techniques from my previous studies, I had to organise my notes and other written materials in a way that I can retrieve the relevant information quickly to answer an examination question. This is where the sticky notes and page markers come in handy. They can also serve as *aide memoir* to prompt you of the concepts and principles that you have learned. This strategy was particularly helpful for me because I used colour-code scheme depending on the nature of the principles or materials. I would use bright colours for important information. For example, I used pink and red sticky page markers for High Court decisions and legislation. Pink and red because they are the major, authoritative sources of law in Australia. I used blue and green for legal concepts and principles. I would also make a one-page summary of a chapter using diagrams and flowcharts (discussed in Rule 5). Then, I would stick that page with either a white or black page marker or a sticky note (don't use coloured markers for summary pages). The one-page summary will be very helpful when for whatever reason, your mind goes blank at the examination or when everything else fails. You just go to this easy to spot one-pager, because it only has either a white or black page marker, and you'll have the summary of the topic in two seconds. This will bring you back to your composure.

Just a tip about using sticky notes and page makers— don't overuse them. You don't want the edges of your notes covered with markers to a point where it's impossible to look for something. It defeats the very purpose of why we use them.

If your examination is closed book and you're not allowed to bring any written materials, you can still use sticky notes and page markers on your notes when preparing for the examination during revision period. As I mentioned in Chapter 8, you can put sticky notes strategically around the house including your bedroom and bathroom, where you can easily see them. They will prompt you to recall important concepts and principles on your way to the kitchen or shower. That daily exposure to these sticky notes creates an entry on your long-term memory. Also, try to make the font look funny or interesting on your sticky notes. The more it stands out, the more likely that you remember them. The words and prompts have corresponding index card versions (Rule 12 about index cards) which contain the explanation of those words. So, every time you see the sticky note try to recall the explanation of that word or phrase. If you can't, then review the index card. You can also associate an image or a story (Rule 11) with the key word or phrase that can facilitate the process of recalling the explanation. So, master this process—glance at the prompt, recall the associated image or story then explain. Repeat this process for as long as you can and pretty soon, it will be etched on your long-term memory. This is similar to how big brands use logos, trademarks and catchphrases to increase customer awareness by associating the brand with good quality apparel or shoes, delicious food or environmentally friendly car. Then there is constant daily exposure on billboards, posters, brochures, TV and internet ads. People see them everywhere, every day. The more exposure they get, the more people associate those logos, trademarks and catchphrases with the messages these big brand companies want to convey.

Now, with page markers, you need to stick them as you go through and read the textbook and reading materials. Allocating a separate task to put all your page markers in one session is not a very efficient process. If you read the pages four weeks ago and you are putting the all the page markers just now, you would have already forgotten what pages things are.

Below are more tips and comments about using sticky notes and page markers. Feel free to implement these and modify them to your own liking.

1. Use multi-coloured pens. Red for vital information, yellow for import information, blue for general principles, etc.
2. Buy smooth writing pens that suit your style of writing. For example, I found BIC pens smooth. A smooth pen affects the speed of your writing. This is particularly important during examinations.
3. Matte page markers and sticky notes are easy to write on compared to glossy ones, but the glossy ones last longer. I used a combination of both. Just make sure to use pens that have a sharper point or tip when writing on glossy markers.
4. Make use of your iPhone Notes app or Sticky Notes app on Windows 10 to augment the use of physical sticky notes. For example, I would save some terms and phrases in my notes on my iPhone while on the go. Once I get home, I would make physical sticky notes for my bedroom or bathroom.
5. Make use of the top and bottom edges of your notes and other written materials if you run out of room on the right-hand side of the pages. In saying this, try to optimise the gaps between markers. Don't leave wide spaces between markers.

6. Have sticky tape handy. You don't want the page markers to fall off. Check them before the examination if they are still intact.

7. The use of sticky notes and page markers on textbooks are not as effective as using them on your own notes. You tend to remember your own understanding of the concepts and principles than the explanation in the textbook. Though, it doesn't hurt if you put page markers for each chapter in the textbook, just in case you need to flick through the pages during an examination.

8. Make use of the different types of sticky notes out there based on size, colour or type of paper (matte or glossy). You can create rules for yourself to use only a specific colour or size depending on the nature or importance of information. Be consistent with your rules across all subjects. Your brain will thank you for it. You don't want to get confused during an examination. For example, if your rule is to use red sticky notes for important information for one subject, make sure to use the rule for your other subjects.

9. Sometimes I would stick a note or two on an empty section of the page if I wanted to scribble words, create diagrams or drawings that come into my mind about the topic. If they don't make sense, I discard them later. If they are helpful, then I leave them there. Often the brain remembers playful drawings better than texts.

10. You can also get creative with your sticky notes by cutting out different shapes such as stars, triangles, spheres, zigzags and diamonds.

11. My pencil case or pouch had all the little things that I might need while studying at the library such as coloured pens, pencils, an eraser, highlighters, coloured sticky notes, sticky tape, phone cable charger, Panadol or Paracetamol tablets, small pair of scissors, earphones, muesli bar, tissues, USB flash drive and some coins for vending machines.

12. Bookmarks can be helpful, but they are not as effective as sticky notes and page markers.

13. You can sort your notes based on the order of the topics outlined in the subject guide and the corresponding page markers but remember the examination questions don't care about the order of the topics as learned in class. The first question can be about the last topic discussed in class.

14. One strategy you can use about your notes and page markers is to number all the pages including any legislation printouts or diagrams. Then you create a table of contents with subsections. You can create two versions of table of contents. One is sorted alphabetically and another by the page number. So, during examination, you just look for the topic related to the question from the table of contents and you'll have the page number. You can almost do without the page markers if you are going to make use of the table of contents this way.

15. The principle behind page markers is so you can easily and quickly find what you are looking for during examinations or assessments. If you can think of other ways or even combine the techniques in this book with your own, to even make it quicker for you to find the pages, then by all means do them.

RULE 10: EXPLAIN WHAT YOU
LEARNED TO SOMEONE

After you learned a bunch of concepts and principles, try to find a friend or someone who is willing to listen while you explain in your own words what you learned. This is based on the Feynman Technique. This activity will force you to recall the things you have learned and test whether or not you understood them. You don't even need to get out of the house. With all the technology these days, you can set up Zoom meetings or Skype calls. If you can't find someone, you can instead make a summary of what you learned using PowerPoint. PowerPoint because you can categorise your thoughts quickly into groups of concepts and principles per slide using key words and phrases. Do it like you're preparing for a presentation. Don't put too many words on the slides. Just make a short description of the concepts. Don't write them in a Word document. You can expound them later on once you've jotted down the basic skeletal make-up of the ideas. The important thing at this point is to extract the basic information from your memory of what you understand about the topic. If you really need to put your insights and interpretation of the ideas, then make use of the notes and comments in PowerPoint. Don't create a separate file. You want to put everything in one place. You don't want to have too many files and lose track of which ones relate to which chapter or topic. After you've done the slides, you can go back to your reading materials and compare if your understanding of the concepts and principles are accurate. This is also the time when you evaluate your progress and whether or not you have to allocate additional time to read your materials again to understand them fully.

Explaining to someone is probably better than the PowerPoint summary option because the other person is actively listening and is also able to ask questions if something doesn't make sense. You can go even further where you do both the explaining and also the

PowerPoint summary, if you have the time to do it. It sounds like an overkill doing both but it's not completely a bad idea. For example, you can prepare the PowerPoint summary before you call your friend. You will gain confidence because you understand the ideas that you are trying to explain. You also don't do a lot of umming and erring on the call because you have already thought the ideas through. You will save time. Then later on in the semester you can use the slides to review for the assessment.

Explaining the concepts that you just learned to someone forces you to structure your thoughts in a coherent and systematic way with the hope that you will be understood. This activity alone is already a good preparation for the assessment because you already know how to organise your thoughts and arguments in a way that anyone can understand. An interesting option that you might consider is to become a tutor or mentor. This option might be limited because you would normally need to have satisfactorily passed the subject to prove that you actually understood the concepts and the principles taught in the subject. This means that you wouldn't normally become a tutor while you are still undertaking the subject but if there's a way to do it, it's a great strategy. One of its benefits is putting yourself in a position that forces you to understand the topics in advance so you can explain them to your tutees or mentees; and you earn some extra money too. If you can handle that extra outside pressure, for example a tutorial every Thursday night after class, then it's a good way to incorporate this rule into your weekly routine. There are probably other ways you can implement this rule in your weekly schedule other than becoming a mentor, so you'll have to examine your current weekly activities. You just need to ensure that whatever you decide to implement that it will be effective enough to force you to actually do it.

If you want to increase your chances of recalling what you learned, do something that will force you to actually remember it. For example, try to write down what you learned after a couple of days, then another after five days, then after a week or two and lastly after a couple or a few months. This is the principle behind Ebbinghaus Forgetting Curve that if you don't make any attempt to recall or retain what you learned, then you will eventually lose it. So, you need to make attempts to recall what you learned within specified time intervals that suit you. You just need to be consistent. You might need to set up reminders on your smartphone or computer for the different time intervals. When those reminder alarms go off, don't just snooze or dismiss them without doing the tasks. I'm guilty of this that's why I try to find alternative ways where I put myself in a position that forces me to do the activities. It could be a no-review-no-go-home Wednesday at 6:30 pm; or a Starbucks Thursday night only Salted-Caramel-Frappuccino-review; or a Saturday night only Malaysian-restaurant-review.

Now, when you do the actual recalling process, you can use different ways. You can use the PowerPoint summary technique as described previously; you can also review the key words and phrases on your sticky notes and page markers as explained in Rule 9; and the use of flash cards as explained in Rule 12.

Another option if you don't or can't do any of the above activities is to make a recording of yourself summarising what you learned using your Voice Memo app on your iPhone. When you listen to your recording and it seems to be making sense, then you're probably on the right track. One good benefit about this approach is you can keep recording yourself until you sound confident that you understand the concepts yourself from your own recording; whereas when you're talking to friends, you can't expect them to listen to you over and over again until you sound like you really know what you're talking about. They expect you know exactly what you're taking about in the first place.

A strategy to make the recalling process easier and efficient is to write down a key concept, principle, words or phrases on one side (prompt side) of an index card as you study them, and the explanation on the other. When you review, you don't need to go through the textbook or materials again. All you need to do is glance at the key words and phrases on your index cards and try to explain them in your own words before turning over for the correct explanation. This would be the equivalent of the PowerPoint summary described previously. We will discuss more about the use of index or flash cards in Chapter 12. The main point of these activities is to review or recall what you've learned as many times as you can in different time intervals—days, weeks and months. Repetition is the key if you want to etch something on your long-term memory. Just note that repetition in this context means repeating what you already understand as opposed to just regurgitating what your textbook says without really understanding what it means.

Another strategy to test your understanding is to have a group discussion with people who have more knowledge or experience than you. They can engage more productively, and you will gain a deeper understanding of the topic. Some of these people may have actually put the ideas that you're trying to explain in practice and not just learned them from textbooks. Their learning from those experiences provides them with a more wholistic understanding of an idea because they have learned both the theoretical and practical aspects. When having a group discussion, just be mindful of the reaction of the people in the group because depending on what topics you're discussing, some of them may find some comments, opinions, reactions or interpretations offensive. They may not be willing to listen to you or other people in the group because they are already fixed to a certain idea or belief and they're not willing to accept or listen to any ideas that can potentially make their long-held beliefs look invalid or unacceptable. They become defensive and the discussion sounds like it's becoming a heated argument. This is not healthy. When you think that you are about to reach this point of the discussion and is becoming a heated argument, it is better to discontinue. The whole point of this activity is for you to gain a better understanding of the topics, not to persuade or engage someone in an argument. That's why it is important to pick the people you trust, willing to listen to what you have to say and ready to give you constructive criticism. The whole discussion will be a wholesome and productive experience. If you're just going to put yourself in unnecessarily awkward and stressful situations by having this group discussion, then you might as well just do the PowerPoint and Voice Memo strategies. Engaging in a debate or a heated argument requires a different set of tools to deal with different kinds of people and discussing different kinds of topics. Those tools are beyond the scope of this book.

We don't want to get side-tracked here, though. Keep your goal in mind—explain how you understand the topics. Recall what you learned after a few days, after a few weeks and then after a few months. In the next chapter we will discuss about the strategy of creating stories or memory castles that will enhance your recollection of things. For now, it is important to get into the habit of recalling things by explaining or creating a summary after a number of specified time intervals.

RULE 11: CREATE A **STORY**

Memory champions use memory palaces and journey techniques. They create a story that involves a journey in a palace to connect images that represent objects, people, numbers, a deck of cards or any other piece of information that they want to memorise. It is easier to recall a story than a bunch of words or a string of numbers. How many stories can you recall right now? Stories from your childhood perhaps or some crazy stories that your friends told you years ago about their trip to Europe. Compare that to say your bank account number or your best friend's mobile phone number. Notice also that stories involve an interaction of objects, places and people. We store images and movements in our head. They are alive in our minds. So, even after a few years you still remember them. So why not convert the concepts and principles that we learn at school into images and movements then conjure up a story that will connect those images. Make the story sound crazy and it will even be easier to remember.

Even though we know these things to be true and that people remember events and stories, we're not taught at school about these and how to use memory techniques and ways on how to retain information. We're just given lots of information and teachers expect students to remember them. They don't equip you with tools to store information effectively in your brain. You'll have to figure them out on your own. Meanwhile, the assessments are due in a few weeks and the examinations are just around the corner. You have no choice but to cram because you don't have a lot of time. It's like a trap that they've systematically put in place with no hope of escape.

Rather than spending a lot of time complaining and pointing out the things to improve in the education system, it's probably better to address the system gaps yourself and find your own ways of learning. Once you've proven that your ways are effective, share them to others.

This is one of the reasons why and how this book was developed. I needed to focus on things that I could control and writing this book was one of them. Attempting to change the educational system seems like a mammoth undertaking anyway; and even if you start allocating resources and time to try and change it, you still need to go through the proper channels. That can take years and without guarantee of a favourable result. I'm not saying that it's not worth the time and effort. If you believe that you can change things through this channel and you're passionate about pursuing changes in the system, then by all means go for it; but this is not something that I would do myself. I'd rather dedicate my efforts and time in developing tools and materials that will help students develop effective ways of learning. The results are more predictable, and the benefits will presumably follow because I have used the learning techniques myself.

Anyway, back to memory palace and creating stories. This skill takes time to develop depending on how much effort you put in. It all depends on you. You can probably achieve the results in no time if you are dedicated enough to get this skill mastered. Just be mindful that this exercise may take a while the first time you do it, so have patience. Once you get past the first hurdle and after using it for a couple of topics, the next ones wouldn't be as hard. I wish I have fully utilised the benefit of memory palaces in the early years of university. I was living in a very small studio apartment near university during law school, so my memory palace or house was very limited. I had to start using the university library and then also my old previous house in lieu of my tiny apartment as memory palaces. I didn't have a consistent memory palace. I was using one place for one topic and another place for another topic. It was hard for me to keep track. I didn't have a set of criteria to go by to decide which house to use in a particular situation. Based on these shortcomings, I recommend that you pick a medium sized house to be your memory palace that you are familiar with. Ideally, you would use your own house because you know it inside and out. Then again, not everyone has a good-sized house to be a sufficient memory palace. You could be like me living in a tiny studio apartment, and that's not the best memory palace to use. If you're in that similar situation, you can go find a four-bedroom house with two bathrooms, double garage and a large backyard. It could be a display home that you've been to or a house featured on a YouTube channel about houses. Familiarise yourself with the house, know every corner, every furniture, the furnishings and appliances. Once you know the house inside and out, you can start selecting images of things and famous people that represent numbers, words, phrases or phonetic sounds. With numbers for example, you can use the image of a wand to represent the number 1 because it looks and sounds like it; a swan for number 2 because it looks like it; handcuffs for number 3; sail on a boat for number 4; a hook for number 5; trunk of an elephant for number 6; and so on. Pick something that you think best represents a number that you can easily visualise. So, if you want to memorise your PIN of 251463 for example, you will create a crazy story that goes something like this:

> A **swan** was caught by a **hook** that is tied to a **wand**. Then a **boat with a sail** came to the rescue. It was carrying an elephant. It stretched its **trunk** with **handcuffs** dangling at its tip.

If you want to use the four-bedroom house journey to memorise the same PIN, then it would go something like this:

> A **swan** appeared at my front door. I let it inside the house. It walked straight to the kitchen then looked up to the **hook** where I put my golden **wand**. I turned on the TV to entertain the swan. The batman movie was on with Christian Bale. The scene was when he planned to disappear while **sailing on a boat**. During the TV commercial, an elephant with a huge **trunk** was reaching for some **handcuffs** from the policeman's waist.

Obviously, if it's something like your PIN, you will probably always remember it because you use it all the time but if you have to memorise something straight away, then this memory technique can help you. If you want to know more about memory palaces, journey and other techniques that memory champions use, look up Dominic O'Brien who is an eight-time World Memory Champion.

I used a lot of stories during law school. Often, the cases themselves elicit interesting responses from the readers. I also still remember, even after law school, stories mentioned in the lectures such as the classic case of *Carlill v Carbolic Smoke Ball Company* where I visualised Mrs Carlill using the smoke balls from the smoke ball company and the smoke was all over her house with the hope of developing immunity from the flu as promised by the company. Instead, she got sick and started coughing. The company effectively broke their promise to give the user immunity from the flu. Therefore, they were liable. Another famous case is called *Donoghue v Stevenson* where Mrs Donoghue who was at a café with a friend, ordered a Scottish ice cream float, a mix of ice cream and ginger beer. When the rest of the ginger beer was poured into the tumbler with ice cream, a decomposed snail floated out of the bottle. Mrs Donoghue already drank some of the ice cream float. She fell ill and complained of abdominal pain. She was required to consult a doctor and was admitted to an infirmary. The ginger beer was manufactured by David Stevenson. We'll skip the other details but basically, it was claimed and held that Stevenson had a duty of care as the manufacturer because it was reasonably foreseeable that failure to ensure the safety of the product would lead to harm to consumers (in this case to ensure that snails did not get into the ginger beer bottles) and that Stevenson breached this duty. Anyway, the point of this case is that I'll always remember this case as the 'ginger beer and snail' story. There are other details in the whole story that I skipped here but if you look up this case online, you will find the story very interesting, something that you will always remember.

It was easier for me to remember cases because they always had stories to tell. The more crazy, funny or interesting the stories are, the more chances that I'd remember them. If I had to remember a piece of legislation which is a whole bunch of text, I would try to find a case that has a good story relating to that section in the legislation. Otherwise, I would just pick the salient information from that section and create a story out of that.

In implementing this rule, you will have to improvise and use whatever information you have or things that you already know and somehow connect them to whatever information you want to store in your brain. It may be hard to do it at first because it's not something that we're trained to do but the more often you do this, the better you will become.

RULE 12: USE INDEX OR FLASH CARDS
FOR KEY WORDS AND PHRASES

This is probably one of the simplest and quickest yet one of the most effective and efficient techniques that you can easily implement. People use index cards for various reasons and in different ways but in general, the way I would use them is to write down key concepts, principles, words or phrases on one side (prompt side A) and the explanation on the other (side B). So, the prompt key word on side A and the explanation on side B. This is very handy during review period because all you have to do is flick through the cards. If you forget a concept, you can just easily turn the flash card over for the explanation. You don't need to go through the textbook and materials again. This will save you a lot of time particularly if you are reviewing the concepts from the first few weeks of the semester because by the end of the teaching period, you would have already forgotten where the concepts and principles are explained in your materials. One typical scenario during revision or review period is having a tall pile of books and reading materials for all your subjects and looking at them makes you feel dizzy. You're thinking: gosh, what am going to do? Well, if you have those flash cards handy, you just pull them out and go through each of them, and there's your review.

The idea of using index or flash cards is to have small and manageable chunks of information represented in an even smaller scale that your brain can easily absorb. You can also make use of the Leitner system where you classify the cards based on the answers to the review questions. Correct answers can be classified and reviewed less frequently while incorrect answers should be reviewed more frequently.

This last rule about flash cards is related to Rule 9 about sticky notes and page markers where you write a word or a phrase to prompt or trigger concepts, principles and ideas in your mind that are associated with that word or phrase. Let's use the phrase *'elements of a contract'* as an example. You write this on the flash card with big writing using a permanent marker. On the other side of the flash card, you list the elements of a contract such as agreement, intention, consideration, capacity and formalities (for example, sale of land must be in writing).

FRONT SIDE (A)

elements of a contract

BACK SIDE (B)

1. Agreement
2. Intention
3. Consideration
4. Capacity
5. Formality (like sale of land)

You will need to do these flash cards as you read the textbook or reading materials when the ideas are still fresh in your mind. After a day or two, review the flash cards by looking at side A and see if you can recall the elements of a contract. Do this again after a week and then after a month or two. You can put more explanation on side B if you need to. The explanation should be brief to fit side B of the flash card but sufficient to understand the concepts. Sometimes if the concepts are too complex to be described in just a few sentences, then you need to use an extra flash card or two. Once you have the flash cards sorted for every concept or topic that you have studied, you don't need to go through the textbook and other reading materials again.

Index or flash cards come in different colours so you can make a colour code system. For example, pink or orange is for the important or main principles; yellow for the exceptions or sub-principles; blue for examples or application of the main principles; and white for examples or application of the exceptions. Be consistent with your colour code system across all your subjects to avoid confusion.

The cards also come in different sizes so make use of them. For example, you can use the big-sized ones for complex concepts as you need more room for explanation and small cards for relatively simple concepts.

Another tip I can give you is to write the textbook page number on the corner of the index card where the concepts and explanations are extracted from. Just in case you need to clarify something or if your written explanation is incomplete, you can easily go back to the source.

Now, since we save most things on our smartphones these days, you can take photos of your flash cards and save them to your OneDrive or Google Drive where you can easily access them. It's actually a great idea to have them on your phone because you don't necessarily carry the flash cards with you all the time, but you always have your smartphone wherever you go. While you wait for your train home or your next class, you just pull out your smartphone and review your flash cards. Just be mindful of how you store the softcopies of the flash cards and try not to mix them with your other photos unless you have a separate folder for them. Often, you spend more time trying to find and retrieve the information you saved because you don't have a systematic and consistent way of storing them. Alternatively, you can download an app from Apple Store or Google Play. It would be much more seamless and efficient if you have an app just for the purpose of flash cards or index cards. This would suit those who are always on the go and don't have time to do the physical flash cards. However, if you have an open book examination and you're not allowed to use electronic devices, then you either have to print those flash cards you created on the app or transfer them onto the physical cards that you can bring when you take the examination. One disadvantage if you do it this way is you will only have a small window of time to familiarise yourself with the physical flash cards before the examination compared to creating them right at the start of the semester.

Below are more examples about the use of flash cards.

FRONT SIDE (A)

Goods and Services Tax (GST)

BACK SIDE (B)

-Is a broad-based tax or value added tax of 10% on most goods and services sold and consumed in Australia, with some exemptions such as food and healthcare

-Legal definition is in the legislation *A New Tax System (Goods and Services Tax) Act 1999*, section 195-1 and then 7-1:

1. GST is payable on taxable supplies* and taxable importations; and

2. Entitlements to input tax credits arise on creditable acquisitions and creditable importations.

*Taxable supply is defined in s 9-5:

1. You make a supply for consideration; and

2. Supply is made in the ordinary course or furtherance of an enterprise that you carry on; and

3. The supply is connected with indirect tax zone; and

4. You are registered or required to be registered.

It is not a taxable supply if the supply is GST-free or input taxed.

17

Notice the number at the bottom right corner of side B. This is the page number of my reading materials and printouts where I extracted the meaning of GST from. If I need to create more flash cards relating to GST, I can just go to page 17 of my materials. As GST is a such a complex and broad-based tax, it might require a couple more flash cards to further explain the other elements of the definition. Examples of goods and services that are taxable as well as those that are exempt will also help illustrate the concepts behind the definition, so that would probably require two more flash cards.

FRONT SIDE (A)

GST-free products and services

BACK SIDE (B)

Most basic food

Some education courses including course materials

Some medical and health care services and some medicines

Some childcare services

Some religious services

Water and sewerage

International transport

Sales via duty-free shops

Exports

Sale of a business as a going concern

Farmland

18

Printed in the United States
By Bookmasters